AF326611

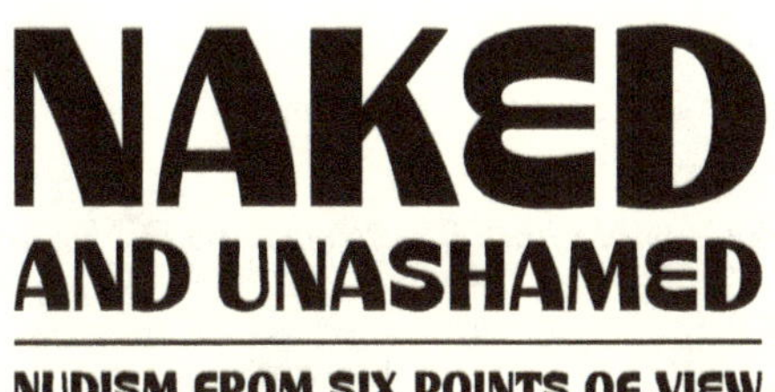

NAKED AND UNASHAMED

NUDISM FROM SIX POINTS OF VIEW

By the same author

The Naked Truth about Nudism

It's Only Natural: The Philosophy of Nudism

available from
wolfbaitbooks.com

First published in 1934
This edition published in 2024
by Wolfbait Books
www.wolfbait.co.uk

A CIP record for this book is available from the British Library
ISBN: 978-1-917298-00-1 (hardback)
ISBN: 978-1-917298-01-8 (ebook)

NAKED
AND UNASHAMED

NUDISM FROM SIX POINTS OF VIEW

By William Welby

Introduction by Tim Forcer

Photographs by Stephen Glass

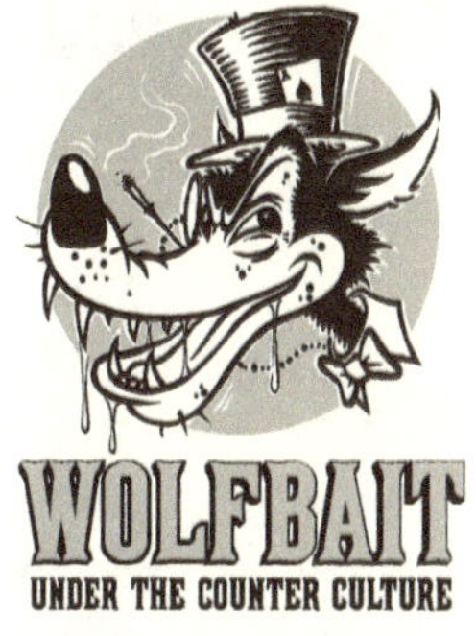

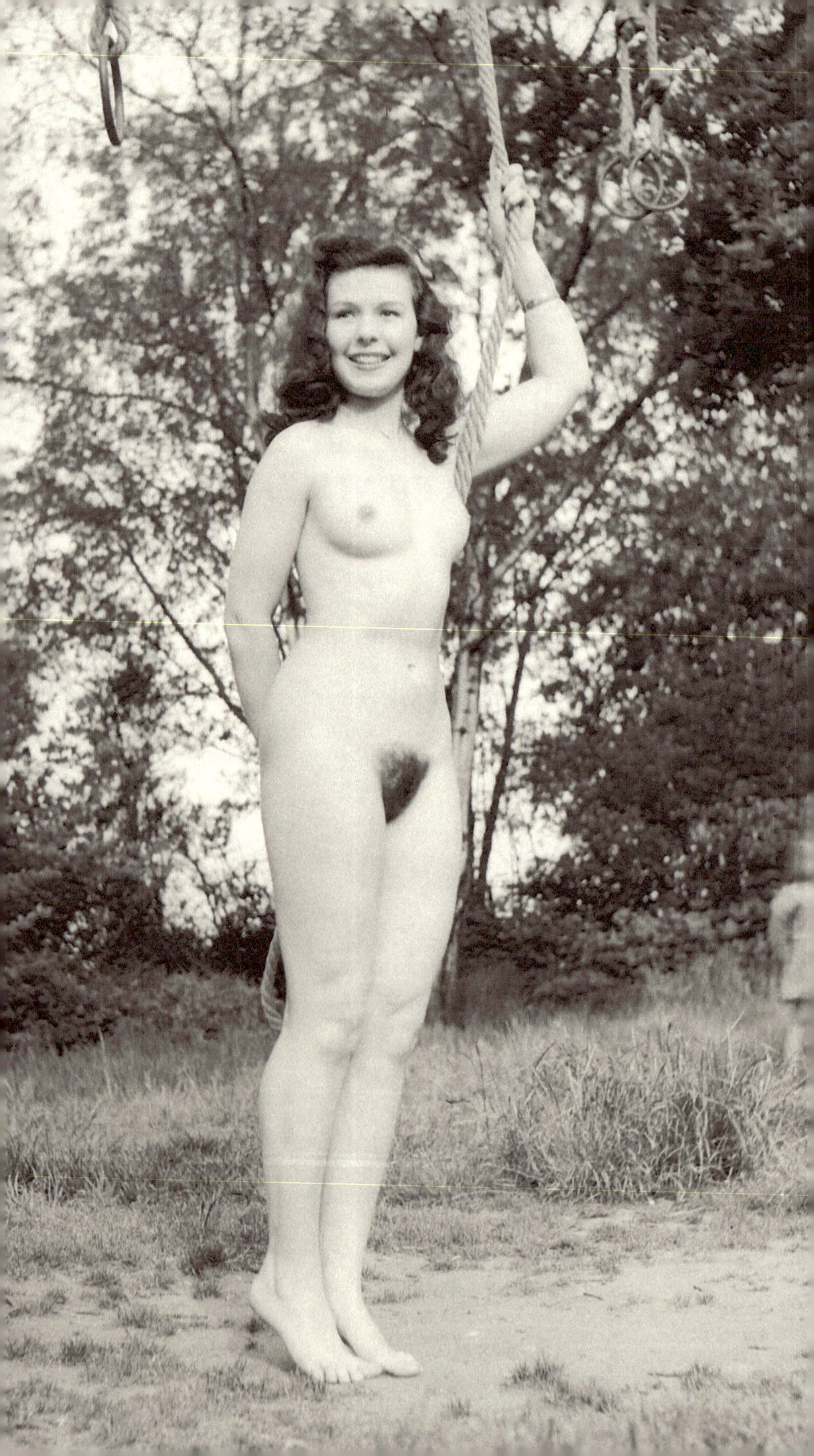

Contents

Left: *Eternal Youth*. Iseult Macaskie at Spielplatz circa 1948.

Illustrations
by Stephen Glass

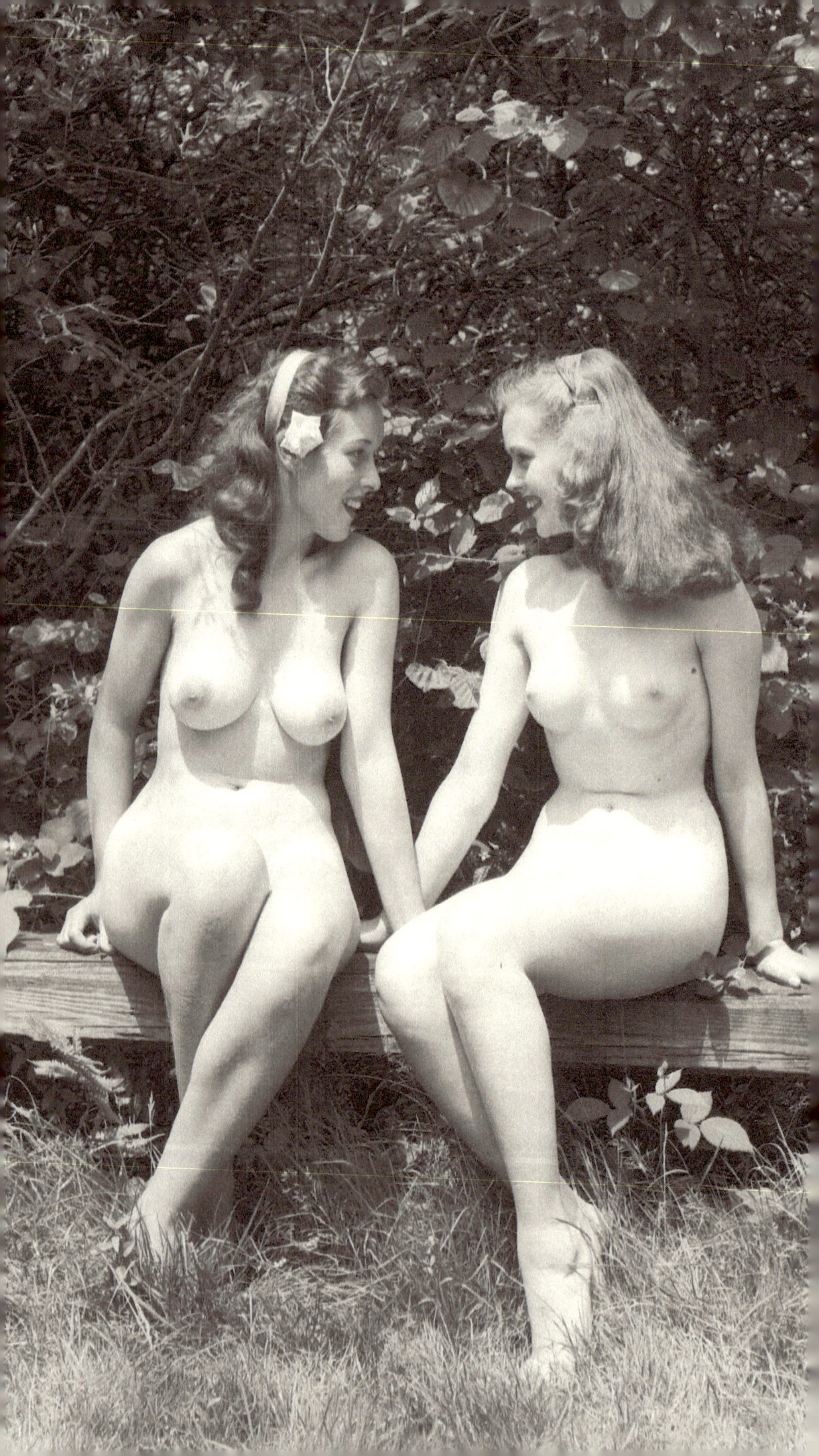

Foreword

THE PERIOD BETWEEN the two world wars saw great upheaval in European society. Political and social structures changed. There were booms and busts, and motor and air transport transformed the economies of many countries. Against this backdrop of turmoil, Germany's *Freikörperkultur* movement expanded, stimulating the creation of nudist groups in other European nations. In England, the first clubs were founded from 1924, and in the 1930s formal associations were set up, while magazines and books featuring social nudity became available.

William Welby was born in 1883 in Canterbury, Kent. He spent his early working life as an auctioneer's clerk in London and on a Canadian farm, after which he became an advertising copywriter. Following World War I, he progressed to the position of advertising manager. Advertising is a profession that relies on the power of words to present information simply and clearly and in the best possible light. In his writing on nudism, Welby usually avoided being overly evangelical, and instead, would set out the facts and arguments for the reader to consider – although it was clear what he thought the conclusion should be.

A surprising element of this objective aspiration is that Welby did not experience social nudity until after he had written *Naked and Unashamed*, his first book on the subject. That fact is declared, along with a report on his first visit to

Left: *Making Friends*. Mina Felgate (right).

a nudist club, in the preface to the book's second edition. The re-publication was necessary because the first edition had been "exhausted in three or four weeks". Together with the favourable comments the book received, this prompted Welby to try nudism for himself. I feel obliged to point out that there was only a month between the publication of the first and second editions in July and August 1934!

Naked and Unashamed was illustrated with 15 full-page illustrations from naturist magazines, evenly split between classic female studies and mixed groups, the subjects uniformly slim and fit (unfortunately, rights issues mean those specific images cannot be reproduced in this new edition). In his chapter "The Æsthetic Point of View", Welby says that people "suffering from deformities… would not wish to expose these," and that association with "members of a fine physique" will encourage the less fit to "acquire… shapeliness and grace… if they will only take the necessary steps". These days, inclusivity and acceptance are implicit or even explicit in the stated aims and objectives of naturist organisations.

Of course, that is just one of many changes in attitudes towards nudity – Welby provides a review of these across cultures and history in Chapter I, to give background to his own arguments that social nudity is healthy in mind, body and spirit. Of the "Six Points of View", Welby considers the moral one to be the most important. In Chapter II and elsewhere he points out that there is a difference between nudity and sex, and the naked body is not intrinsically erotic. These and other points are well known to nudists, but they must have been quite novel to many in his intended readership. In the chapter on health, Welby contends that skimpy clothing is not only titillating but unhealthy in various ways. He states that for the optimum production of hormones, the genitals must be exposed to sunlight. Similarly, he asserts that full body visibility is good for mental health: not just for adult nudists but also their nudist children, who will avoid neuroses caused by misunderstandings about sex, reproduction and puberty.

If the arguments – summarised in Welby's concluding "The Commonsense Point of View" – are commonplace today, why bother reading this book? I think it is helpful to understand where organised naturism came from, and how it was seen in a society where it was not only a novelty but an imported novelty. Until the early 1930s, not one British author had published a book about nudism: what information there was came primarily from isolated articles in health magazines and from foreign publications.

Welby's three books were among several nudist titles published by Thorsons. These included *Among the Nudists* by US authors Frances and Mason Merrill. That was reprinted in 2006, and is even available as an ebook, but until recently anyone interested in contemporary British writing on the subject had to search the second-hand market, where the books' prices can be quite high. A few months ago, naturist author Will Forest posted on goodreads.com about his Brazilian friend Jorge Bandeira, who had translated Welby's books into Portuguese. Bandeira had found the books helpful and wanted his compatriots to be able to access them too. This meant the works were more readily available in Brazil than in the UK, and I wondered if anything could be done to reissue them here. Fortunately, I was aware that Wolfbait

Books had already republished other early naturist titles, so I approached its publisher Yahya El-Droubie to see if he would consider this project. He agreed and asked me to contribute this foreword. I hope you find the book interesting, with its mix of attitudes from a man who was in his late teens when Queen Victoria died. While some of Welby's perspectives may feel rooted in the past, others possess a timeless quality that remains relevant even today.

Tim Forcer
of *H&E Naturist*

Author's Preface
to the Second Edition

I HAVE BEEN asked to write a preface to this Second Edition of my little book and this gives me the opportunity to extend the considerations laid before the reader in the First Edition. Although I wrote the book because I felt there was a real need for it (I think it is the only presentation of Nudism of its kind yet published), I was not prepared for the remarkable success which it has achieved. For a First Edition exhausted in three or four weeks may be considered a remarkable success, I think. I have learnt a good deal from the publication of the book without receiving one adverse comment or criticism. The principal effect has been to make me realise that I am not nearly so "advanced" in thought as I imagined. I know a certain number of people who I thought might quite likely be shocked to hear that I had written on such a subject as "Nudism." I have been agreeably disappointed. After approaching the subject delicately with talk about a book I had written on "Sunbathing," I discovered that so far from being shocked, they were genuinely interested and after reading the book expressed nothing but praise for it. Those whom I most expected to regard it as improper proved entirely void of such a thought. It just did not occur to them; which shows how much depends upon a point of view. St. Paul's saying to Titus, "Unto the pure all things are pure," has become so hackneyed as to be regarded as cant, but surely here is a practical proof of its truth; and confirmation of my belief that no wholesome-minded person should find anything indecent or shameful in the human body without clothes. Another incident was enlightening. My wife showed the book to a friend and his wife rather anticipating disapproval. To her surprise they both liked it and the husband volunteered the information that one of his clients took his wife to a Nudist colony for a month's holiday every year. And we had doubted if these friends knew what Nudism really meant! One criticism I met was: — "Do you practise what you preach? What Nudist Society do *you* belong to?" When I said that I belonged to no Society and did not actually practise Nudism myself, I was greeted with an ironic smile. Until I pointed out that I did not "preach" nudism in my book. My introduction states clearly that it is not intended to be used "as propaganda either for or against Nudism." The object of the book was to place facts and considerations before the reader upon which a sound judgment could be formed without bias or prejudice. Had I been a Nudist myself how easy it would have been to claim that I "had an axe to grind" and that I was cunningly trying to convert people to my own ways. English justice is of such high quality that it might be possible for an English Judge to try a case in which his personal predilections were involved and his judgment would be accepted with respect; but I doubt if the same freedom would be allowed to a writer on a controversial subject. If the conclusions drawn from my book favour Nudism, it is because the facts themselves form a sound argument and the illogical and illusory ideas which have been built up around the question of Nudity are shown for what they are. I do not want to convert anyone to nudism. I want them to please themselves; but I do also want them to understand just what it all means before forming an opinion. I have endeavoured to do what a good judge does—assist the jury in arriving at a sound verdict by marshalling the facts and summing up the evidence. It occurred to me, however, that first-hand experience of Nudist activities might prove both useful and interesting and, having received an invitation from the Secretary of what seems to me to be one of the most efficient and satisfactory Clubs in this country, I gladly availed myself of the opportunity to meet the Nudists on their native heath," so to speak. I think a brief account of my experiences and reactions will be welcomed by the reader. When I received the invitation and decided to accept it, my wife thought she would like to accompany me. I believed that, holding the views I do, I could take off my clothes and enter the Nudist Colony without the slightest embarrassment; but when I told my wife that she would no doubt have to do the same, she began to vacillate. She thinks "it is quite all right for those who like it." In the abstract she is a "pro-nudist," but when it came to a question of personal participation she was a little doubtful. In writing to the Secretary asking if I might bring my wife, I pointed out this difficulty and asked if, in the event of her feeling either bashful or chilly, she could wear a bathing costume. His reply was characteristic: "She can wear anything she likes. I can safely promise this from experience, as she will soon be so embarrassed wearing clothes in the company of the naked that her only anxiety will be to take them off." Nevertheless, to be prepared for emergencies we took with us a bathing costume for my wife and a pair of swimming "trunks" which I wear in my garden. While we were on our way, I certainly did rather wonder if at the last moment I should feel any qualms; but my wife told me she had resolutely set her mind against contemplation of the "ordeal" in case it might induce a state of panic. Our fears were groundless. After a long and rather tiring journey from Essex to Dorset we found ourselves at the home of the Secretary on the edge of the New Forest. Mutual introductions were effected in a matter of seconds and after a few minutes' chat in his office we felt quite at home and as though we were old friends. We were fortunate in having an ideal day for our initiation. There was no question of being chilly. A clear blue sky and a warm sun with the scent of pines and heather all around us ensured the right atmosphere and our host proved as charming as his letters had led me to expect. He explained that his wife had already gone over to the Club as she felt "such a glorious afternoon was too good to waste." He proposed that we should go along right away and a few minutes' car ride brought us to a gate inside which several cars were parked. Our friend led us towards a screen of small, bushy trees reinforced with wattles about seven feet high. He opened a small door with a Yale key and we entered what was virtually a new world. Not that there was anything to see, save trees and bushes, but as the door clicked to behind us I felt in some subtle way a different person. Following a woodland path we came to a clearing with a canvas bathing pool in the centre, some deck chairs and a Pavilion with the centre part thrown open. As we stood on the steps a lady came out of the woods and was introduced as the wife of our host. If I had been in any danger of embarrassment it was dissipated then. No hostess could have received guests more reassuringly and although we were clothed and she was not, it did not seem to make the slightest difference. She took my wife to the ladies' dressing room while my host and I shed our clothes in an adjoining cubicle. As we came out I saw my wife chatting freely with her new friend—perfectly at ease. By this time a few more members had come into the clearing and we exchanged nods and greetings just as though we had been there for years. The two ladies wandered off through the woods and I was piloted round the domain by the Secretary. I do not propose to give a detailed description of the Club. That may be done in a later book when I have had experience of a number of clubs. It is just the initial impressions of my wife and myself which I wish to record, because we are very ordinary people and I think it may be assumed that readers of this book who are ordinary people would feel just as we did. Previously I had considered Nudism mainly from the physical angle. For the last year or two I have enjoyed the sensation of a sun-soaked skin and I have had practical proof of the benefits to be derived from it; but here I felt a sort of spiritual uplift difficult to describe. I felt in some way "superior" to my earlier self and to all those poor creatures muffled up in material clothes and psychological prejudices. After a complete inspection of the resources of the club, during which we chatted and smoked just as we might have done in any ordinary club, we all met again in the main clearing and had tea sitting in deck chairs amongst the other members. Then we were taken to one of the sports courts and played some vigorous games of "Tennikoit" or Ring Tennis. Those who have never played without clothes cannot realise what a difference this makes. Apart from the freedom of movement allowed, there is a sort of "out of school" feeling which doubles the zest of the players. Altogether it was a most enjoyable experience and though I had kept a perfectly open mind when writing my book, I am now definitely pro-nudist."

William Welby
Essex, August, 1934

Introduction

A few years ago considerable courage and optimism would have been needed to write and publish, in popular form, a book on the cult of Nakedness or "Nudism." But the movement has grown so rapidly and spread so widely that it is desirable for everyone to have at least sufficient knowledge of the subject for intelligent understanding. It is not the purpose of this little book to provide a learned discourse, plentifully peppered with footnotes and references to great works to be found in the British Museum and other strongholds of the studious. It is not intended to be used as a textbook by students. Nor is it a tract to be used as propaganda either for or against Nudism. Rather it is planned to set out, in a simple and concise way, information and reflections which will assist each reader to form a sensible judgment free from fallacies and prejudices. Some people may regard the question as a moral one; others from the viewpoint of health, or beauty or religion. In the following pages the subject will be considered from each individual point of view under the headings:—

The Historical Point of View,
The Moral Point of View,
The Health Point of View,
The Psychological Point of View
The Æsthetic Point of View,

and the concluding chapter will review all that has .preceded it from the "Commonsense Point of View." While no attempt has been made to deal with the whole subject exhaustively, a task neither possible nor desirable in the present volume, each chapter covers the ground with which it deals comprehensively and lucidly. In the conclusion a general summary of the points discussed, with observations upon their trend, will assist the reader to analyse his (or her) own reactions to them and so to form a rational and independent individual judgment of Nudism and the Nudists.

CHAPTER I

The Historical Point of View

ALTHOUGH WE ARE told that after eating the fruit of the Forbidden Tree, Adam and Eve "became aware of their nakedness and were ashamed," scientific research shows that body-covering first came about not through any sense of shame, but solely for protection from the weather and temperature. At this very moment there are thousands of men and women in tropical countries who wear no vestige of clothing of any kind and yet are quite unashamed. Indeed, travellers and students of Ethnology have emphasised the fact, over and over again, that amongst tribes who live in a state of complete nakedness, chastity is universal and licentiousness unknown. On the other hand, when climatic conditions call for protection from cold we find the peoples muffled up to the eyes in skins and furs; as for example, the Esquimaux. When man was just an unthinking animal, long before morals and conventions were thought of, he wore clothing of sorts in those parts of the world where his own covering of shaggy hair was found insufficient protection from the cold. But it was a long time before clothing became significant for other reasons. To begin with, he found in it opportunities for exercising his vanity, opportunities not entirely neglected even in the present day, and from this a "sense of clothes," as it were, began to develop.

When clothing came to be worn for purposes of adornment, new ideas were added, and it is a fact that in climates where cold was unknown the sexual parts of the body were the first to be covered. It is a fallacy, however, to suppose that this was done from any sense of shame. The earliest forms of religion were of a sexual nature, and the fact that certain organs were responsible for the reproduction of the race, and so survival, caused them to be regarded as of extreme importance and even as sacred. Therefore, while protection for these organs might be considered eminently desirable, they were also the first to deserve adornment, and in some countries or districts natives may be seen wearing strings of brightly coloured beads, seeds or shells, which actually draw attention to these parts instead of serving to hide them Incidentally, it may be noted that, generally, while the importance of sex is better understood and never underestimated by primitive peoples, the obsessions and perversions common amongst more "civilised" races are practically unknown. Flirting, petting and prostitution are the accessories of a higher form of culture.

As civilisation progressed and life became more complicated all round, clothes gained in importance. The invention of weaving and the improvements which led to finer textures being manufactured made those who could afford it pay greater attention to their apparel until clothes were worn almost as badges of rank. There were two ways in which development advanced. One was concerned almost entirely with form, as in the case of the Greeks, and the other with richness

---

Right: *The Sun-worshipper.*

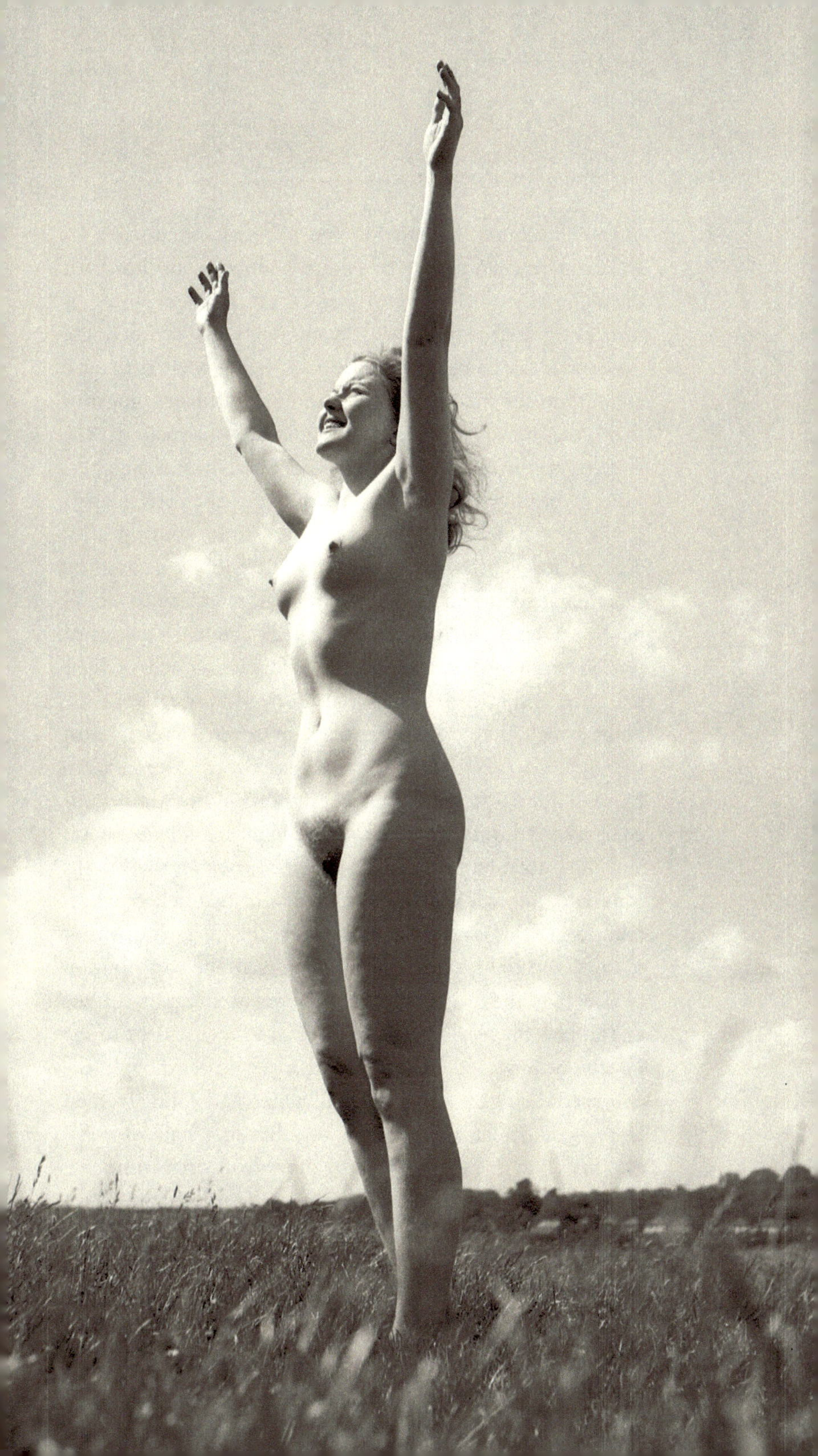

of embellishment, favoured by the Orientals. Even when civilisation reached a state of luxury and grandeur, however, the sight of the naked body was by no means regarded as something indecent. The Orientals, perhaps, scorned the nude form as being insignificant; as being unable to give pleasure to the eye without rich and colourful trappings. In their case, to a great extent, clothes made the man. To the Greeks, on the other hand, the human body was the highest form of beauty, and although they draped themselves artistically in vestments of exquisite texture and colouring, they did not forget the body beneath. Conventions having, by this time, become an accepted part of everyday life, it would have been considered unseemly to walk about the streets or pursue ordinary business in a state of nudity; but in their sculpture and in their games they glorified the beauty of the body, which they exposed entirely or covered merely with such drapery as would serve to enhance the uncovered parts. From childhood to adolescence, physical culture was regarded as a sacred duty, and regular attendance at a gymnasium and the public baths was a matter of course. Yet the Greeks cannot be regarded as barbarians devoid of intellectual attainments. The sagest of philosophers, the most eloquent of orators, and the greatest of statesmen were the contribution of Greece to the future culture of the world. In art, in science and in law, the world of today owes an immense debt to the Greece of long ago. And these highly cultured people encouraged their girls and boys, young men and young women to practice games and exercises together in a state of nudity—partly to ensure freedom of movement unencumbered with irksome garments; partly, we may assume, that the sight of the beautiful physique of some would impel the admiration and emulation of others less well favoured.

As time went on, fashions in dress grew more and more elaborate—and so did conventions. The introduction of Christianity caused a reversal of the Pagan ideas, and from pride in and worship of physical attributes, attempts were made to concentrate upon the spiritual. To this end the physical was made to appear gross and unholy, and as far as sex was concerned, even unclean. The early Christians were urged to "mortify the flesh," and hermits shut themselves up in caves and endeavoured to concentrate their minds on spiritual things by keeping apart from things physical. This may have acted as a check upon the licentiousness and decadence which the luxury lovers of Rome had begun to spread, but it seems a pity that endeavours should be made to cure excesses in one direction by fresh excesses in another. History shows only too plainly that Christianity has been used as an excuse for cruelties and intolerances which would certainly have been abhorred by its Founder. Most conventions have served a useful purpose when first established and many retain their usefulness for long after. Whether the convention regarding sex and unclothed bodies is useful or not will not be discussed here, as we are dealing only with the historical viewpoint of nudity. In Europe the disapproval of nudity gradually became general and the exposure of certain parts of the body was regarded at least as indelicate, if not actually sinful, except by people of coarse character. What to the Pagans had been a serious, even sacred, subject was treated with levity and occasional sniggers and giggles when talked of in semisecret by loose-mannered, libidinous groups.

Fashions change with the swing of the pendulum, and the extreme asceticism of the early Christians was succeeded by a certain laxity in later periods, during which the dress of both women and men was allowed to accentuate, although it covered, the sexual differentiations. In the Middle Ages men wore "cod-pieces" fitted to their sexual organs, and these adjuncts to male attire were included even in the designing of uniforms for soldiers. Obviously, the effect was to emphasise these particular organs, and yet neither the lords nor the ladies of that time suffered the least embarrassment. The latter shared in this freedom from restraint by wearing gowns made of such thin material and fitting so closely that the figure was revealed as frankly as by a modern bathing costume. Lacking either the frankness and sincerity of the pagans or the fanatical righteousness of the Christian reformers, these customs suggest a victory for hypocrisy rather than any delicacy of feeling. At a still later period, Fashion decreed that it was permissible to expose the bosom completely, although this privilege was generally restricted to the higher classes and such occasions as we should to-day call "dressy." Women with beautiful bosoms naturally made the most of such opportunities, and the older and less beautiful consoled themselves by being more modest and feeling more virtuous. No farther back than the Restoration Period it was quite usual for great ladies to have their portraits painted with breasts uncovered, and such portraits may be seen in public picture galleries in most of the great cities of Europe.

It is commonly considered that the reign of Queen Victoria marked the most prudish era in England, and that this was partly due to the fact that she was a Queen; however,

this theory is hardly tenable because, as far as dress was concerned, there was very little difference between England and
any other important country in Europe. And the fact of Eliz-
abeth being a Queen certainly gave rise to no prudishness
during her reign. The prudishness of Victoria's reign may
rather be attributed to the goddess fashion and the fact that
history records alternate reactions from looseness to austerity
and vice versa—as witness the Puritanism which followed
the death of Charles I. and the licentiousness which followed
in its turn when Charles II. was restored to the throne. Be
this as it may, we cannot in our survey overlook some of the
absurd pruderies which were peculiar to Victorianism. It was
deemed scandalous to refer to a woman's leg or a man's trousers. The former could only be designated as a "limb" and
the latter as "unmentionables!" And then the bathing costumes! The younger generation of today gaze with laughter
and incredulity on the ridiculous costumes with their baggy
trousers and voluminous skirts worn by some of the bathing
belles to be seen in old prints, to say nothing of the tent-like
apparatus which was lowered over the ladies who had the te-
merity to bathe at fashionable watering-places in still earlier
days. It must have been impossible to swim in such heavy
and cumbrous attire; but, presumably, swimming would not
have been considered "lady-like" in any case. Mixed bathing,
too, was at first regarded with horror, although anything less
likely to give rise to erotic feelings than the shapeless and
bedraggled appearance of such females would be difficult to
imagine. For evening dress, however, a far more generous
display of feminine charms was allowed. The whole of the

shoulders could be exposed without exciting comment, and quite a large proportion of the bust came within the bounds of decency.

In "The Naughty 'Nineties" a great deal was made of exhibiting the beauty of the female form by the wearing of tights. These were confined to wear on the stage by ballet girls, music-hall artists and principal boys in pantomimes. In Paris, at such notorious rendezvous as the "Moulin Rouge" and "Bal Tabarin," special dancers gave exhibitions of the "cancan" and so-called quadrilles clad in billowy dresses beneath which were clouds of foamy underskirts, and when, as occurred frequently in these dances, one leg was waved high in the air, the skirts fell back and showed a few inches of bare thigh between the glossy black-silk stockings and the filmy drawers.

No very startling change took place between then and the Great War (1914–1918) when first "hobble-skirts" were worn, followed by the "Directoire" dress. The "hobble-skirt" was really a sheath-like dress which fitted tightly to the figure right down to the ankles—hence the nickname "hobble," the stride being confined very much as a horse is "hobbled" to prevent it straying. The "Directoire" was copied from the style worn at the time of the "Directory" in Paris during the latter part of the first French Revolution. Its principal characteristic was a slit down the side which revealed the leg as the women walked, and it was originally inspired by the garments worn by the Spartan girls who were consequently known to the ancient Greeks as "thigh-showers."

Due, probably, to the manifold activities of women and girls during the War, skirts became shorter and shorter until they attained knee-length—certainly far more hygienic than the long dresses which had hitherto swept along the ground, gathering dirt and germs at every step. Towards the end of the War, a great deal of latitude was allowed in evening dress. "Backless" frocks leaving the whole of the back bare down to the waist were common, and in some more daring instances an inch or so below the waist. On the stage bare legs became the vogue in light musical shows and "revues," and it was not very long after this that small triangular slips (covering much less than a native loin-cloth) with brassieres to contain the breasts were accepted as being perfectly decent and proper to the public eye. For bathing, women's costumes became smaller and tighter until "shorts" and brassieres, similar to those worn on the stage, were adopted as "sensible" for sea- and sun-bathing and men needed only a pair of shorts, with the upper part of the body quite bare.

In the meantime, first in Germany, later in France, America and England, the cult of "Nudism" or complete freedom from clothing was revived, although this was indulged only in specially reserved "sun-parks" open to members of Nudist Clubs and Associations.

Before closing this chapter, some mention should perhaps be made of the Scandinavian custom of bathing in the nude. In Norway, Sweden and Finland, this has been common in villages and outlying parts for many generations; possibly it has been followed uninterruptedly since Pagan times. Du Chaillu, the traveller, referred to his own experiences when visiting these countries in 1880. He describes the village bath-house as a sort of large barn with a stone fire-place in the centre, which was made nearly red hot and then dowsed with buckets of cold water until the bath-house was filled with steam. It was customary for the whole village to meet here on Sundays in a perfectly nude state, both sexes of all ages being indiscriminately mixed and taking turns in switching each other with bundles of twigs to accelerate the circulation of the blood. Apparently, there were no dressing rooms and everyone went to and from the bath in the same state of nudity. It speaks volumes about the hardiness of these people when Du Chaillu refers to their coming straight out from the steam-bath and rolling in the snow on their way home! Apart from innocent fun of this kind, the ceremony was carried out with the utmost decorum and the introduction of a stranger caused no embarrassment whatever.

In this chapter we have carefully refrained from comments on moral or other effects, because it is the purpose of the book to treat each facet of the subject quite independently; but in the preceding pages we have given a general outline of how the draping or undraping of the human body has been regarded from primitive times up to the present day in order that we may consider other aspects free from the prejudices or misunderstandings which so often affect judgments on matters with which we are insufficiently acquainted. We can now proceed to discuss the next most important phase, i.e., "The Moral Point of View."

CHAPTER II

The Moral Point of View

IT IS REALLY rather curious that morals and clothes should be supposed to be indissolubly bound together. We have already pointed out that amongst the most chaste races of the world are those who wear no clothing at all. Why, then, should so many people assume that the unclothed body must inspire lewd feelings and break down all moral restraint? Artists are believed to be unmoral as a class and to indulge in promiscuous relationships with their female models. Henri Murger's famous sketches of the Paris "Latin Quarter" probably did much to make this view popular and to establish a tradition followed by later writers. But those who mix with artists know that, on the whole, they are just as moral and respectable as any other class of men. Some of them may carry on intrigues with members of the opposite sex, but so do some stockbrokers and solicitors. There is no foundation for the idea that artists, through viewing nude models, are overcome with passion and cast aside all social and moral decency to satisfy an insensate lust. It might just as easily be thought that doctors, owing to their intimacies with their female patients (which are of a more detailed nature than those of the artist), would give themselves up to unbridled licence and be unsafe to trust with a cherished wife or beloved daughter.

What happens is this: to the artist the nude figure upon the model's dais is a subject to be interpreted in pigment,

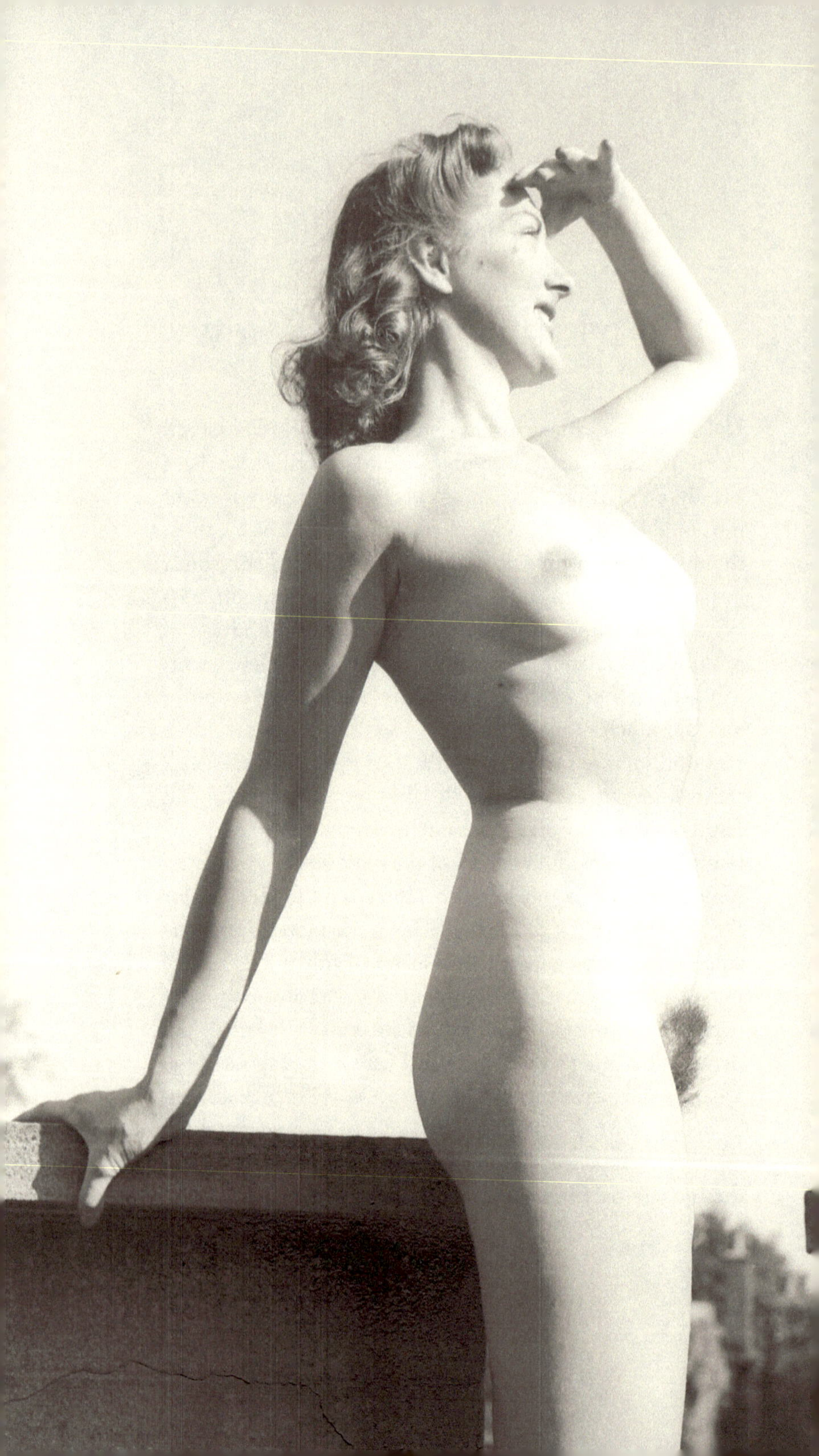

and all the faculties of the artist are concentrated on the endeavour to bring this interpretation as near to his ideal as
possible. Models, too, can be, and are, as well-behaved as
girls in other walks of life and very often come from families which have followed the same profession for generations.
Those unfamiliar with the nude may be excited by curiosity
and the atmosphere of daring, which has been artificially and
quite unwarrantably built up around the idea of the exposed
body of the opposite sex; but this is of a nature similar to
the curiosity of schoolboys and is due mainly to ignorance
or inexperience. There are, of course, Paul Prys and Peeping
Toms who gain a sort of illicit thrill at the thought of viewing
nudity in a furtive way. But these people are not normal any
more than a drunkard or a congenital thief. Such people will
generally be found to have a marked distaste for exposing
their own bodies in the presence of others—unless they are
also imbued with an exhibitionist tendency, which is just another abnormality. Really, there is nothing disgusting about
the human body any more than about the body of an animal.
The sight of a dog or horse or cow in trousers or skirt would
be the height of absurdity, because we are all quite used to
seeing them in their natural state.

It must be, then, purely a matter of convention which has
placed the stigma of indecency upon the nude human body.
Why is this stigma not attached to statues and pictures? One
answer may be that the organs of sex are usually omitted; so
the indecency must be on account of these organs. But in
many statues and some pictures, in public galleries, the male

---

Left: *Ship Ahoy!*

organs at least are shown quite plainly, and in those instances where a fig-leaf is employed, the effect is to attract attention simultaneously with the suggestion that here is something obscene. If it is indecent for sex to be displayed, it can be only a question of convention; and all conventions have arisen, in the first place at least, for practical reasons, so that we must seek for a practical reason in this case.

In the previous chapter, it was shown that the early Christians in their endeavour to exalt spirituality cast a slur upon things physical. This was not unnatural because the spirit and the body are upon different planes and it is not easy to harmonise the two. The Mahatmas and holy men of India are able to subdue the physical side of their natures to such an extent that their spiritual powers approach the marvellous. It is possible, with extraordinary willpower, to reduce the physical claims of the body until cold, heat, hunger and pain become almost nonexistent. The Orientals, particularly in India, seem able to carry this spiritualisation to a point far beyond what is possible to a European. But it is possible for everyone to increase spirituality through the suppression of physical desires. The fanatical reformers of the time were evidently aware of this and planned their campaigns on this basis. The most powerful of physical desires being that of sex. This became the first and most obvious point for attack. Phallic worship and the glorification of sex in general, physical strength and physical beauty had to be dethroned to make way for the new religion of the spirit. The methods employed were no less logical and no more deceptive than those used by present-day politicians. The only criticism that can be made is that a certain sense of proportion was lacking. The intentions were good, the ultimate object was praiseworthy, and the reformers themselves were, in the main, absolutely sincere.

In the course of time, the original reasons for most conventions are forgotten and the conventions are obeyed just because they are conventions. The average mind is not highly analytical, and the fact that certain ideas have been generally accepted over a long period is sufficient to prevent most people from questioning them. Unfortunately, many fallacies come into existence in this way. One such fallacy is that the sight of the nude body gives rise to erotic feelings. This is so far from being true that experts in eroticism like the Orientals ridicule such an idea. The lightly veiled or semi-exposed body certainly has an erotic tendency. This is due to complicated psychological processes; the air of mystery, the appeal to curiosity, the suggestion of delights temporarily withheld and the actual enhancing of bodily beauty with draperies and ornaments. There is also the association of ideas. The popular idea that there is something wicked, daring, thrilling, in viewing the exposed body of the opposite sex gives rise to sensations which have nothing to do with the body itself. Otherwise a classical statue might have the same effect. But in a normal, intelligent person, feelings of this kind are dispersed immediately. Nudity is regarded in a plain, commonsense light. For this reason, the so-called nudists who practise sunbathing and physical exercises in slips and brassieres are open to criticism. Such practice is not only inconsistent, but it actually attracts attention to the differences in sex and becomes suggestive in the same way as the stage-shows which are produced with this object in view. It is not nudism; it is not conventionally respectable. It is liable to turn the thoughts of onlookers into inquisitive and erotic channels and is therefore definitely undesirable from the moral point of view.

Can, then, groups of mixed sexes carry on social intercourse in a state of nudity without encouraging immoral thoughts or actions? Of course they can. They are doing it at the present moment. The existing Nudist Societies in Germany, France, Italy, America and England, include amongst their members men and women of unimpeachable respectability. Clergymen, doctors, barristers, military and naval officers, and women of corresponding social classes will be found in every reputable society. It may be argued—it is, in fact, argued by Nudists themselves—that the intermingling of the sexes without clothing definitely dispels the pruriency and pseudo eroticism fostered and stimulated by mock-modesty. At these gatherings, which are mostly in the open air, it is usual for the members to spend the greater part of their time in physical exercises or in games of a nature to improve the physique. It is also usual to have children and their parents present. Under such conditions, there can hardly be any encouragement to erotic or unseemly behaviour.

With a new and unconventional cult, however, there is always the danger of the introduction of crooks and cranks. Requiring leisure and money for its exercise and so attracting well-to-do people, it opens avenues of exploitation by those parasites of society who live by duping the simple and the credulous. The very fact that Nudism is regarded by the less broad-minded with suspicion or ridicule protects the exploiter against the risk of legal action by his dupes, as their self-respect and sensitiveness will make them wish to avoid publicity. There is also the possibility of still less desirable types entering the field with the object of pandering to degenerates who would neither be able to nor wish to join a genuine society. Probably such a class would very quickly attract the attention of the police and be treated in exactly the same way as keepers of disorderly houses. It is unlikely that people with improper motives would try to join the genuine societies, for, as we have said, Paul Prys and Peeping Toms are disinclined to come out into the open and show themselves, and their very prurience gives rise to a certain amount of mock-modesty which is totally at variance with the spirit of Nudism.

Another question which might be raised is whether association in the nude could bring about a familiarity between members and such discussions upon sex as to lead to illicit relations at other times and other places. This is possible. The removal of barriers, the lifting of restraint, would leave individual conduct freer from the calls of convention as would any contact with broadening influences quite apart from Nudism. To be a Nudist at all presupposes that the individual is disinclined to be bound to popular opinions. To represent this as a charge of immorality against Nudism would be flagrantly unfair. All we are really concerned with here is whether the nude body is likely to serve as a stimulant to erotic desires, whether people gathered together in a nude state may be expected to cast aside their ideas of decency and whether they would join a Nudist association with such objects in view. All the evidence points to the contrary. It can hardly be doubted that a number of persons gathered together, including families, divested of clothing for the purpose of athletic games and exercises, would be far less susceptible to erotic urgings than a young couple in a darkened cinema at a performance of one of Hollywood's latest exhibitions of "Sex Appeal," or at a music-hall revue where chorus and principals half-reveal their supposed charms, accompanied by sensual music, pseudo love songs and suggestive dances. Nudity, in itself, is not an erotic stimulant, and if it were adopted with such purpose in view, the Societies certainly would not be patronised by respectable people. This is not "begging the question." Reference to books on eroticism and a little logical reflection will support the first contention, and the writings and speeches of well-known people of both sexes will confirm the second. So much for the negative side of the question. It is no great recommendation for a thing to suggest that it is harmless.

The consideration of the positive side is left to subsequent chapters, in which advantages to health and the psychological effects will be dealt with in due course. Whether such advantages exist, whether there is any benefit at all from embracing the Nudist cult, will be purely a matter for individual judgment; but it is first necessary to know how the desire for clothing came about and what cause there might be for deeming the discarding of clothing as immoral in itself or as leading to immorality—immorality, in this case, meaning sexual irregularities, as immoralities like lying and stealing could hardly be affected one way or the other by clothes.

In the next chapter, "The Health Point of View," we may be a little more positive, though we shall endeavour to be no less critical in examining the claims and possibilities of nudism.

CHAPTER III

The Health Point of View

NO ONE CAN remain indifferent to any course which is known to improve or maintain the health of either the individual or the race in general, and the strongest claim that can be made by Nudists is that their policy will, and does, offer a definite aid in this direction. Various reasons may be advanced in support of this argument—some so simple as to be obvious, others more complicated and requiring a knowledge of facts which are not generally known. Everyone knows that fresh air and exercise are essential to health. It will hardly be denied that the majority of people have insufficient of either; although the recently acquired popularity of "hiking" and camping must have affected a great improvement in this respect, especially so far as the younger people are concerned.

Human nature is so constituted that some stimulus is required before any real effort is made even in so important a matter as maintaining good health. It is so much quicker and easier to swallow a tablet or a draught that patent medicines are preferred, on the whole, to more natural mews. To carry out certain mechanical exercises in the solitude of a bedroom or bathroom, regularly and over a long period, needs a degree of enthusiasm and determination possessed by few. The ingenious Americans made a bid to overcome this drawback by the production of gramophone records providing music and oral instructions so that the "daily dozen" could be carried out in privacy with a stimulating atmosphere similar to that of a gymnasium or institution. It is quite certain, however, that physical exercises carried out by groups are pleasanter and more efficacious than those performed alone, and the Nudists have this point in their favour. In a Nudist community made up of enthusiasts, there is a natural incentive to exercise and enjoy fresh air. But, it may be argued, this could be obtained by joining an ordinary tennis-club or similar organisation. So it could, but not, perhaps, with the same glamour or degree of earnestness. And then there is the benefit to be derived from the actual exposure itself.

From very early times it has been realised that we breathe partly through the pores of our skin. There is a legend that a youth taking part in a Roman festival procession was covered with gold-leaf and that he died, or collapsed, through the pores of his skin being sealed. Since then, much more has been learned about the skin and it is now recognised that the skin is an organ in the same sense as, say, the liver or the kidneys. Like the kidneys, it absorbs certain desirable elements required for the health of the body, and like them also it exudes, in the form of perspiration, certain poisons which otherwise would be retained in the blood-stream. The affinity between the blood and the skin being very close indeed. It performs definite and essential functions. It controls the temperature of our bodies. It can absorb certain rays from the sun and store up the vital vitamin "D" to be reabsorbed into the blood as required. Hence the recommendation of sunbathing by celebrated physicians.

Right: *Sunlight and Shadow.*

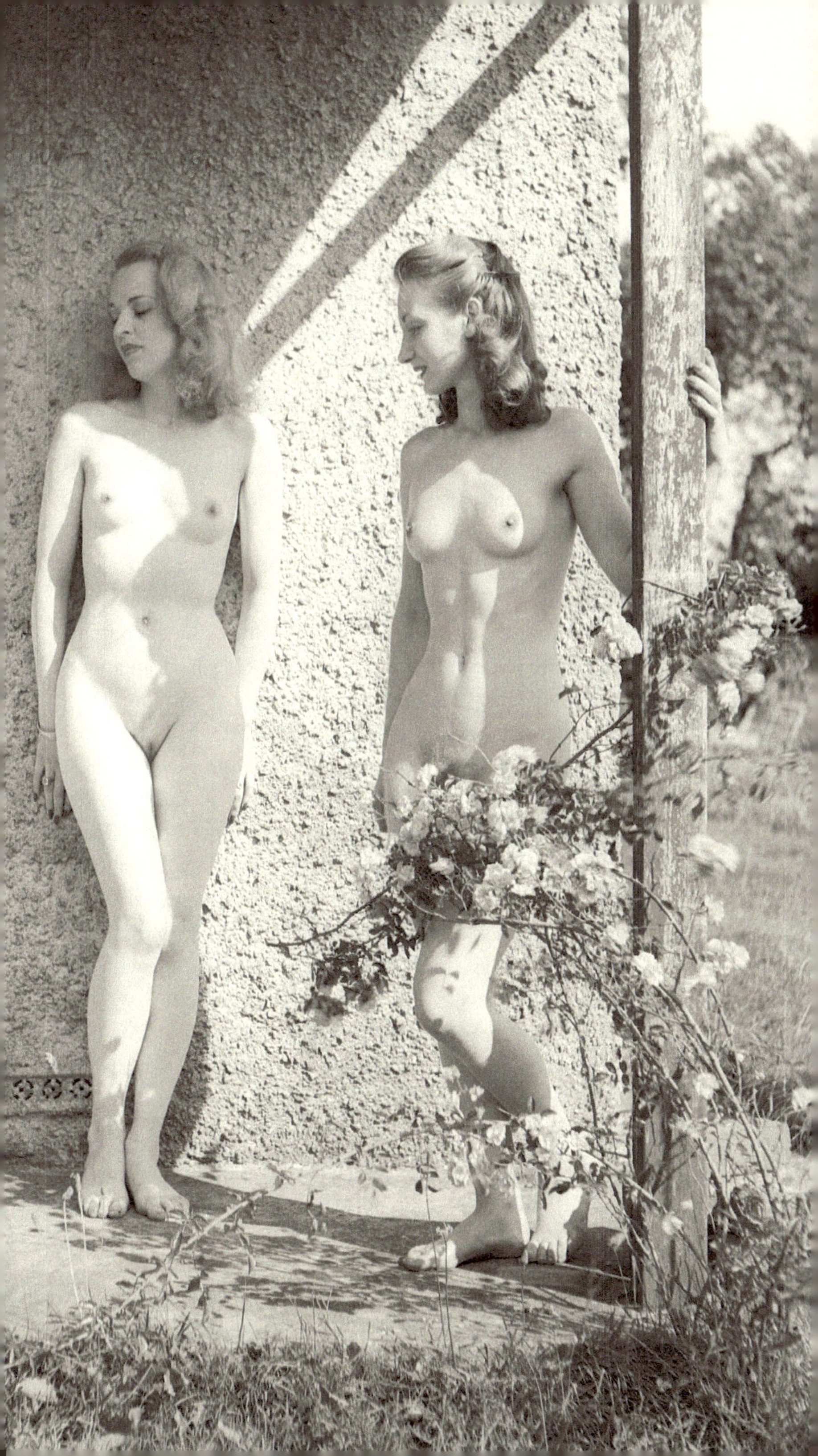

The tonic effects of sun and air upon the skin are indisputable, and in many diseases suitable exposures have been known to effect reliable cures. In Switzerland, where the treatment of tuberculosis is carried out more intensively and on a larger scale than in any other country, complete and almost complete exposure was practised before Nudism as a cult came into existence. So valuable have the ultra-violet rays, in particular, been found that special lamps are manufactured to emit these rays and make it possible for them to be enjoyed indoors or when no sun is visible. The really powerful lamps are employed only under suitable professional direction and the exposures are for very short periods but smaller varieties for home use which, while being of comparatively little value in the treatment of disease, have an appreciable tonic effect, are now becoming quite common. More so in America than in this country.

For the skin to perform its functions properly, it needs exercise just as the muscles do. Exposure to the air tones up the skin and encourages it to do its proper work. Heavy clothing, for this reason, is not healthy. If we try to maintain the temperature of our bodies by clothes, we give the skin less work to do and it becomes inefficient, as does any other organ which is given insufficient use. Comparison with the muscles and the teeth will help to make this clear.

It cannot be doubted, then, that exposure of the skin to light and air is beneficial to health—to some degree essential. This being so, it is only logical to assume that the more skin is exposed the greater the benefit. So the Nudists argue that every bit of the skin should be exposed. This meets with objections in some quarters on the grounds of morality and decency. The semi-nudists believe in all the advantages of exposure, but contend that to cover certain small portions can make very little difference to the total benefit received and that to do so overcomes the objections referred to. We have pointed out in the previous chapter that there is nothing intrinsically immoral or indecent in the nude body. That, in fact, the covering of just those parts which typify sex makes them more conspicuous and therefore may, on a purely rational basis, be considered more indecent. It must, at any rate, induce more self-consciousness. On these grounds alone, complete nudity would seem to have the advantage. But there is a great deal more in it than this.

During recent years, scientists have studied certain ductless glands—that is, glands having no entrance or exit, so to speak, other than through the blood itself. These glands are called "endocrine glands," and manufacture—again putting it rather baldly—the endocrine secretions, which are essential to health and happiness. Two of the principal glands of this kind are the pituitary gland in the brain and the thyroid gland in the neck. Some years ago, when Professor Voronoff announced the results he had achieved by grafting the thyroid gland of an ape upon a human being, much amusement was caused amongst the general public by referring to the thyroid as "monkey gland" and a mistaken impression that such grafting was claimed to make old men into youths and to extend longevity almost indefinitely. Actually, scientists do not make claims of this nature, but the importance of this gland has been definitely established and thyroid extract is now produced by regular manufacturing chemists and used by physicians in the form of injections or capsules to be swallowed by the patient.

Now the sex glands also produce "hormones" or secretions which pass directly into the blood and are of immense importance to health. A deficiency in these secretions causes a lowering of vitality, and the simplest and most satisfactory method of rectifying such a deficiency is by the stimulation and encouragement of the glands themselves. The free access to sunlight or the application of ultraviolet rays is claimed, upon good authority, to have this effect. Ductless glands appear to be particularly susceptible to light treatment, which is used professionally in cases of goitre, an unfortunately rather common disease of the thyroid gland, and in rickets, which is caused by a deficiency of vitamin "D."

This is not a treatise on photo-therapy or light treatment, but enough has been said to show that there is a very definite benefit to be obtained by exposing the sexual organs to sunlight or artificial sunlight. It must be quite clearly understood that we are referring here to the secretions absorbed directly into the blood and not to specifically sexual secretions such as those which are concerned with reproduction. Sunlight may, by generally increasing vitality, act to some extent as an "aphrodisiac" or excitant of sexual impulses, but that is a secondary consideration which will not be discussed here.

Another point to be remembered is that the ultra-violet rays are present during all the hours of daylight. In or near cities or manufacturing towns where the air is polluted with smoke and other vapours, a proportion of these rays is filtered out, and also on foggy or cloudy days. But where the air is perfectly clear, these rays are as powerful in winter as they are in summer, and it is possible to get well tanned, or sunburned, skiing or skating surrounded by the snows of the

Swiss mountains. To some extent the effect of the ultra-violet rays may be even greater owing to reflection by the snow and ice, just as one may get brown more quickly at the seaside during the summer holidays. The sea air has a little to do with this, but the main factors are the clearness of the air and the reflection from the water. Most amateur photographers know that plates and films exposed at the seaside require only about one-half as long an exposure as those exposed inland.

We all know that one can have too much of a good thing and exposure of the body to direct sunlight requires a reasonable amount of discretion. It is most unwise for the unpracticed to expose the whole or the greater part of the body for any length of time. Exposure both in area and duration must be tackled gradually. In the desire to "come back nice and brown" there is often a temptation to lie in the sun and "cook." This generally leads to painful and unsightly blistering, which no creams or emollients can counteract until sufficient time has been given for the skin to heal itself. Nature makes her own provision for protecting the skin from too great a penetration of the ultra-violet rays—if she is given the chance. The so-called "tanning" or "bronzing" is brought about by pigmentation of the skin for the special purpose of shutting out or filtering the rays in excess of what is desirable. This is another instance of the skin functioning to our advantage when allowed to do its proper work. If exposure is confined to merely a few minutes to commence with and gradually increased, this pigmentation will form automatically and prevent not only the blisters and "peeling," but also ill effects upon the liver and the constitution generally which violent and irrational exposures are liable to cause.

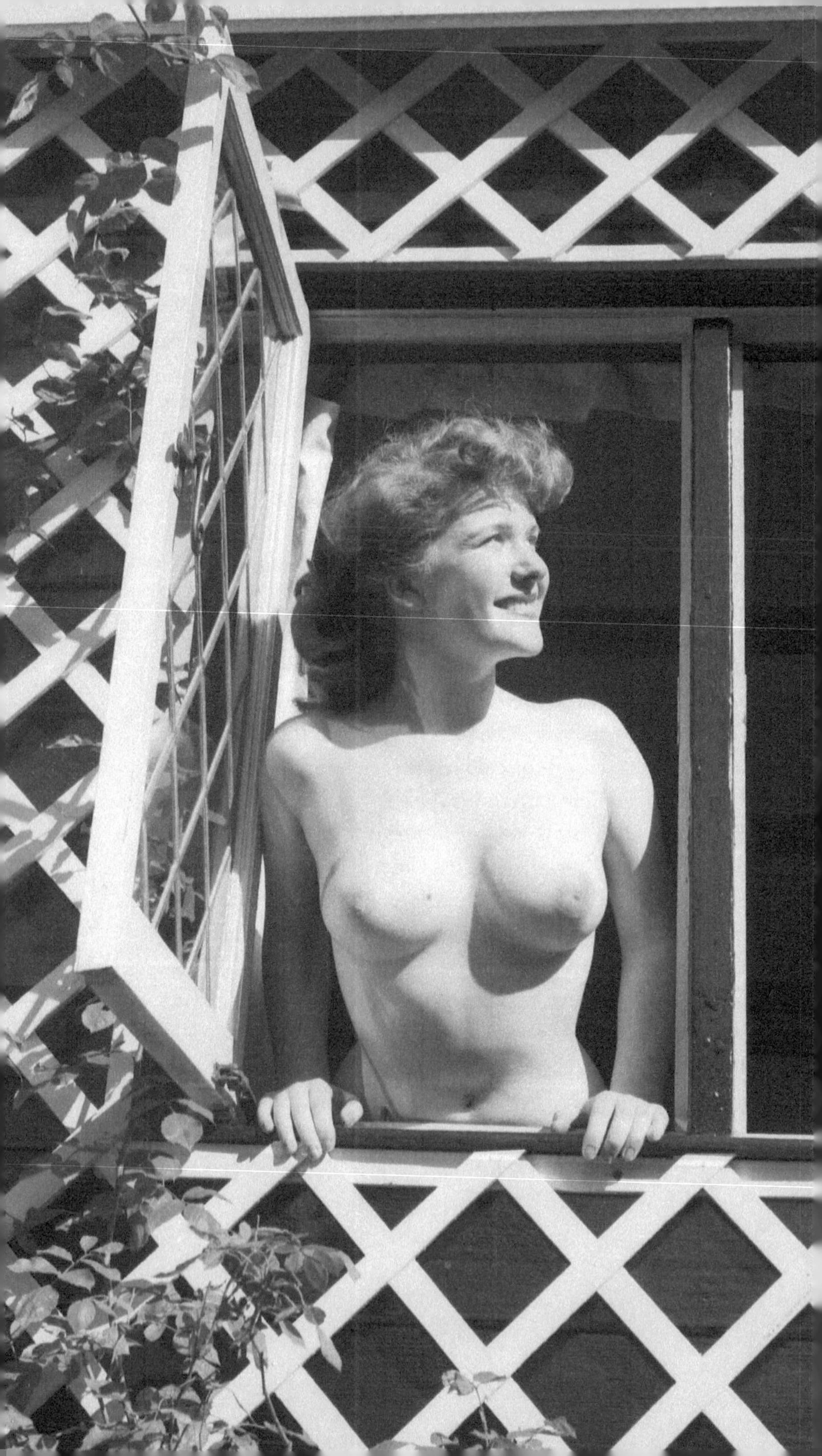

One might as well expect to get well more quickly by taking a whole bottle of medicine at one draught instead of in the regulated doses prescribed by the physician. Exposure is far more beneficial, too, if the body is kept in motion. When lying in one position, the rays are naturally concentrated upon certain portions of the body while other parts receive none at all. Movement makes the exposure more general, and the currents of air act as mild insulation from the infrared or heat rays which are liable to scorch the skin. Vegetable oils are also of value for counteracting the drying effect of these rays, cocoanut oil being preferable to any other.

So much for the advantages and disadvantages of complete exposure, the disadvantages being under personal control and easily avoided with moderate care and common-sense. Nudism does encourage the enjoyment of fresh air and exercise, complete exposure has definite advantages over partial exposure and the claims of the Nudists are, so far, well sustained. There is one criticism still open, however. Why should not complete exposure be enjoyed, but in solitude or in groups of one sex only?

From the purely physical viewpoint, there seems to be no answer to this criticism. It is hard to see how the mixing of the sexes, eliminating all question of eroticism, can have any real physical effect, and there is certainly no reason at all why those who believe in and wish to enjoy the physical advantages should join a Nudist group if they feel any reluctance to associate in the nude with the opposite sex or with any other persons at all. This is a matter of personal taste and

<hr>

Left: *Curves at the Casement.*

conviction. We cannot, however, dismiss the claims of nudism on physical grounds alone. "Man cannot live by bread alone," and consideration of other factors besides the strictly physical must be admitted. Our health and our mental wellbeing are linked up with the comparatively new science of psychology, and we must examine what the psychological effects of Nudism may be and whether they are good or bad or merely nugatory. That is why the next chapter is devoted to "The Psychological Point of View."

CHAPTER IV

The Psychological Point of View

THE ALLIED SCIENCES of medicine, anatomy and physiology were founded some centuries ago, but the science of psychology is of relatively recent origin and has been considerably modified since the advent of psychoanalysis. Psychology being of an abstract nature and dealing with such an intangible subject as the mind is difficult to define and is bound to prove more controversial than the more exact sciences. It has been variously described as the "science of the soul," drawing its name from the Greek "psyche" meaning "soul," the "science of the mind" and the "science of behaviour." The latter is more easy to follow because it is fairly obvious that by studying the actions and reactions of a subject, one can arrive at a fairly accurate conclusion as to what behaviour may be expected under a given set of coincidences and conditions.

In spite of the wide variations of human character, it can be assumed that, with occasional exceptions, a human being will definitely react in a certain way to certain stimuli. To take a very simple example, let us suppose that three men named, respectively, Jones, Smith and Brown, sit talking in a lounge of an hotel when a page boy passes calling the name of a man wanted on the telephone. If that name is Robinson or Wilkins, it will make no impression upon the minds of these three men, and if asked afterwards, all three will probably say that they "did not hear it." On the other hand, if the name called is Jones, Smith or Brown, the individual owning that name is pretty certain to notice it and pay attention to the summons. As another example, let us take a small crowded cinema when a man jumps up in a state of excitement and rushes up the aisle shouting "Fire! Fire!" In this case everyone will take notice, although it does not, of course, follow that everyone will fall into a state of panic. These examples, crude and simple as they are, will serve to illustrate the possibilities of a study of "behaviour" which, being activated by the mind, must also give us an understanding of the mind itself.

The psycho-analysts go very much further than the ordinary psychologist and apply their methods to the treatment of diseases of the mind and nerves. Both Freud, the originator, and his pupil Adler, who later founded a rival school of thought, place the greatest importance upon the influences of sex in the working of the mind. Freudian psycho-analysis is indeed practically based on sex motives and traces nearly all neuroses, or derangement of the nerves, to sexual repressions and inhibitions. It will be seen from this that psychology has a very direct bearing upon Nudism and vice versa. The theory that repressed sexual desires and thoughts are responsible for irritability, depression and other mental and nervous afflictions requires that these repressions must be relieved by bringing them out into the open and either giving them freedom, if that be permissible, or by "sublimation," which is giving them an outlet through another channel.

An old maid, through the repression of her true sexual emotions, may become extravagantly prudish; through her conscious thoughts fighting against those of her subconscious (or as Freud calls it, the "unconscious"), and this leads to nervous and mental derangement. But if these thoughts and feelings are "sublimated" by the concentration of affection upon an adopted child or some creative hobby, the "complex" will be simplified and harmony re-established. It follows, then, that free association of the sexes in a nude state will, by dispersing the feelings of secrecy, hypocrisy and shame which have been "bottled-up" in the mind of the individual, remove or reduce nervous or mental tension which has been caused through curiosity as to the bodies of the opposite sex or through desire to observe these bodies which the subject has repressed under the impression that such desire was disgraceful. We do not, for one moment, suggest that Nudist communities should ever serve as hospitals for neurotics, but such "inhibitions" probably exist in the minds of most people in so mild a form that they might be considered normal. Greater freedom would, perhaps, benefit the nervous system (unrealised by the subject) and make for greater happiness generally.

Let us take the development of sex knowledge in a child.

Years ago, children were told that they were found under gooseberry bushes or brought in the doctor's bag. Subsequently, when their curiosity about the subject grew greater (owing to the natural development of their sexual instincts contemporary with their physical growth) they would find that there was a great deal of mystery attached to "this baby business." They would become anxious to learn more about it, without consciously connecting their curiosity with their own sexual organs in any way. In the course of time, they would learn from older or more precocious children something of the real facts, but all such knowledge would be acquired under a cloud of secrecy and in an atmosphere of furtiveness. It would be treated largely as a joke, but a joke of a rather "wicked" and disgusting nature. With many old-fashioned parents, any evidence of knowledge 'acquired would be severely punished and a "complex" would rise in the mind of the child. The desire to actually observe for itself the sexual organs of the opposite sex would become so strong that it might amount to an obsession, the effects of which would be noticeable later on in adult life. Or the complex might take the opposite form in what is known as "exhibitionism" or "showing off," which is the cause of adults being prosecuted for "indecent exposure."

Early familiarity with the natural form of the opposite sex destroys both curiosity and the sense of shame, and the frankness and comradeship of a Nudist community must help to a more natural attitude in this respect. No doubt the average individual would feel some slight embarrassment on appearing nude amongst a group of strangers or comparative strangers, but this is likely to wear off very quickly. The fact that a number of other people in the same condition appear perfectly at ease, and that a complete lack of curiosity regarding himself (or herself) is obvious, would very soon dispel any sense of awkwardness, and with the fun and excitement of a game of volley-ball or similar exercise self-consciousness would pass away. After this, there would be a sense of freedom of the mind similar to the freedom of the body. In any form of athleticism the encumbrance of ordinary clothing would prove not only irksome and unpleasant, but a real handicap, and it is not unreasonable to suppose that this discarding of clothes, with their subconscious or unconscious effect of repression, would impart a sensation of freedom and lightness to the mind.

The feeling of intimacy which association in the nude must inevitably bring about would make for greater friendliness and give encouragement to the communal spirit. It is impossible to stand on one's dignity or act snobbishly when bereft of the trappings of class or caste. Although we are all schooled, from childhood onwards, to obey and conform to the generally accepted conventions, most of us find a certain delight in ignoring them when suitable occasions offer as on a country picnic or bathing party, or in dressing unconventionally during a holiday. It is a simple psychological fact that we are constantly doing of our own free will and yet reluctantly those things which we have been taught to regard as the "right" things. A child has to be reproved or reprimanded daily for minor solecisms or refractions of the "rules." The adult applies judgment to his (or her) actions before they are committed, and thus a sort of civil war is carried on between his natural impulses and desires and his conventional training. To escape from this conflict of emotions, temporarily, relieves the nervous tension which, if protracted, may cause various degrees of unhappiness or even the common complaint of a "nervous breakdown."

Amongst Nudists there is, as it were, a return to childhood. They meet in the pursuit of health and happiness and a release from at least some of the restraints which may fret and

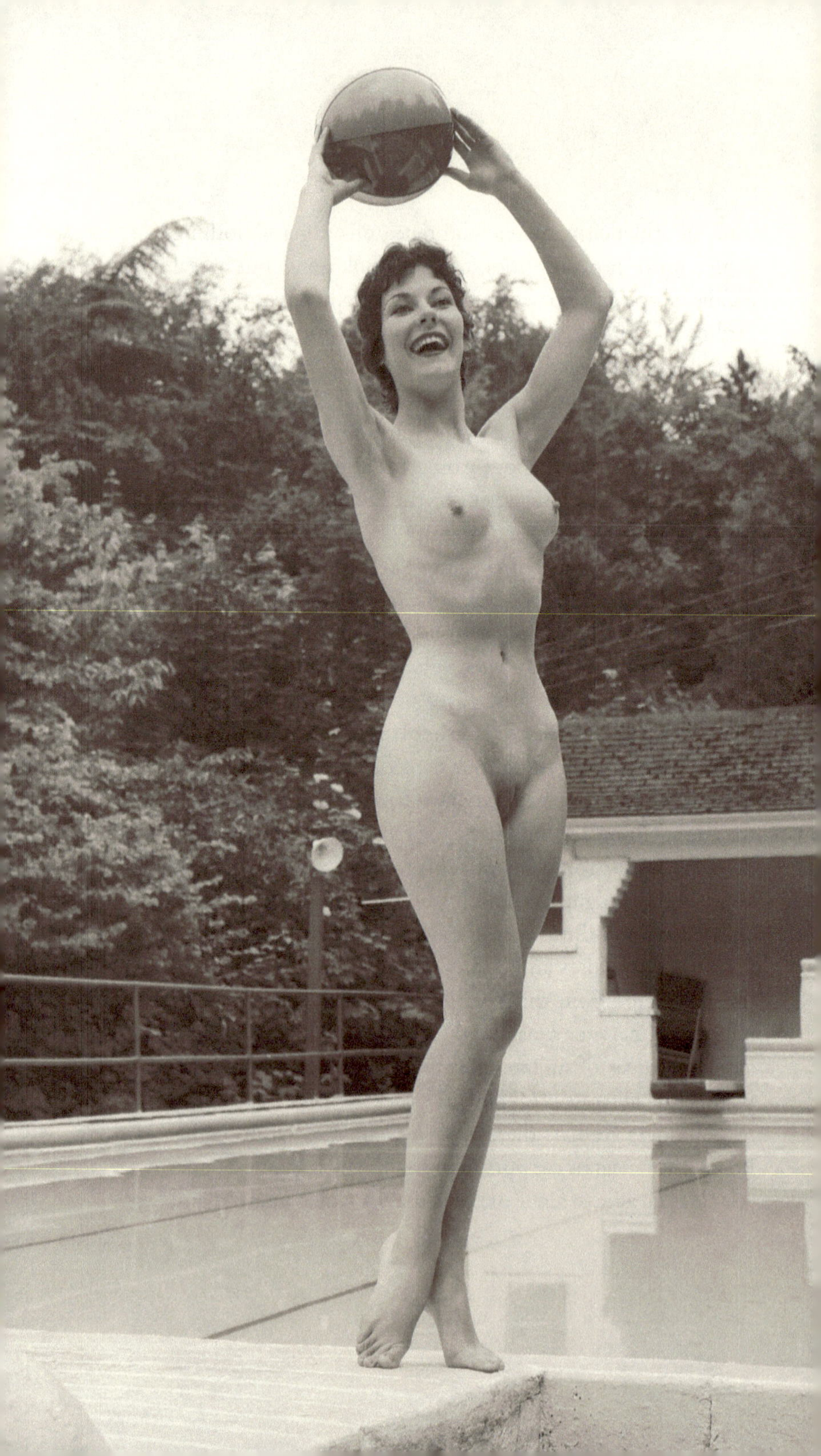

disturb those who are not naturally in harmony with everyday conventions. There is, too, a decided inducement to endeavour to improve the physique. None of us is entirely free from vanity and we choose clothes which we think will set us off to advantage: but without clothes the only alternative is to do what we can to make our bodies more shapely by physical culture with a corresponding improvement in health and strength. The ideal for which everyone should strive is "*Mens sana in corpore sand*," but while everyone would like to have "a sound mind in a sound body," the systematic exercise and training of mind and body receive very little attention from the majority, and those who do take a certain amount of trouble over one frequently ignore the other. The psychological stimulus to more worthy efforts may well be supplied by taking part in Nudist sports, where both mind and body are free and the spirit of emulation is keen. We shall have more to say about this in the next chapter.

The individual temperament must, of course, play an important part. Those of a shy or timid nature may find it difficult to adapt themselves to nudist conditions, or, on the other hand, these conditions may serve to cure them of shyness and timidity and give them self-confidence and enterprise. Some with strict religious convictions may feel they are doing violence to their consciences, which would only add to their mental and nervous disharmony. Others, may find it almost impossible to break down the resistances formed by their early training and environment so that their artificial impulses are stronger than their natural impulses. This is not inconceivable.

Left: *Poolside Playtime*. June Russell at the White House Club near Croydon, Surrey.

All who contemplate experimenting with Nudism must work these things out for themselves, and, above all, make sure before joining any group that it is composed of persons whose characteristics will be readily acceptable.

Age is of but little importance. Young people who have grown up under the broader influences of modern life are naturally more attracted by the movement than older and more conservative people ; but practically all Nudist Societies include members of all ages from small children to men and women of sixty years or more.

Allied with the psychological point of view is the æsthetic point of view, as beauty or ugliness must necessarily have an effect upon the mind, but we have left this to the next chapter in order that we may deal with it in greater detail and avoid any confusion of ideas.

CHAPTER V

The Æsthetic Point of View

BEAUTY IS, AND MUST BE, largely a matter of personal taste influenced by fashion. Architecture, clothes and pictures belong to their respective periods, and, oddly enough, even the beauty of the human body is judged according to time and place. In some parts of the world, beauty is exemplified by distorted lips, as in the case of the "plate-lipped" belles of Uganda, whose lips are gradually distended by the insertion of discs until they are about equal in diameter to an ordinary cheese-plate; or pendulous ears, broad nostrils; or, in China, tiny feet. Even in our own country there have been fashions in physical beauty. Generally, up to the Great War, "feminine curves" have been the criterion of female beauty. So essential was a fullness and roundness of the breasts considered that in the most respectable ladies' journals advertisements were always to be found offering treatments which promised to "develop the bust from six to eight inches." And at one time there was the "bustle," a pad worn across the loins, which was doubtless an unconscious revival of the Greek enthusiasm for "beautiful buttocks" or "eupygia." In the Museo Nazionale at Naples is "Aphrodite Kallipygos," a statue of the goddess in which she is shown with her dress pulled up to the small of her back in order to display her "beautiful buttocks"—

permanent evidence of the esteem in which this part of the female form was held.

Towards the end of the War, feminine curves appear to have become discredited, and the ideal aimed at was a slim, straight, boyish figure. The most probable explanation of this apparent inconsistency is that the freedom and development of eroticism which the war brought about included girls of much younger age than had been considered from this point of view, except by elderly debauchees, in previous years, and that this slimness and straightness suggested a youthfulness which had become more attractive and provocative. However that may be, the pendulum seems to have begun its swing in the opposite direction and feminine curves are returning to favour again.

Although we commenced this chapter with the statement that "beauty is, and must be, largely a matter of personal taste influenced by fashion," there are certain abstract principles of beauty which are immutable. Proportion and balance must always, to some extent, govern all natural ideas of beauty Without any education or training in art, the normal individual is distressed by the sight of anything that is "top-heavy," "bottom-heavy" or "lop-sided." On the other hand, soft and sweeping curves give more pleasure to the eye than straight lines or sharp angles. For this reason, a well-developed body is considered naturally beautiful, and this beauty is emphasised and increased by graceful movements. The well-balanced and proportioned body of an athlete throwing the discus, hurling the javelin, dancing, or even running or jumping, makes a pleasing sight. Over-development or imperfect proportion is not pleasing, as witness the enormous and knobby muscles in photographs of so-called professional strong men. Here is a definite instance of ambitious man endeavouring to "paint the lily" and improve on nature.

Between the extremes of under-development and over-development, we have the average man and woman who are neither unsightly nor worthy of being called physically beautiful. In a gathering of Nudists, we must expect to find all these types and even some who might be classed as unsightly. What is likely to be the effect of seeing all these people without clothes? One person may say: "I would like to join a Nudist organisation if only I could feel that my body was more comely." Another may say: "It would be all right if all the nudists were beautiful, but I should be horrified at the sight of a thin, skinny man or a fat, flabby woman."

Are these attitudes really justified? Were it not for the fact that we are so used to it, we might feel just the same when mixing in a crowd of fully clothed people. In spite of all that may be done by dressmakers and tailors, the thin remain thin and the fat remain fat. Very little amelioration of definite physical defects can be effected even by the cleverest dressmakers and tailors—and only a small minority are sufficiently well-off to patronise their expensive establishments. Those whose duties or pleasures take them to the crowded parts of London or big provincial cities see some thousands of fellow human beings every day; yet how many of these leave any impression at all? A very small proportion indeed; and if questioned on return from a business or pleasure outing of this kind, most of us would find it difficult to describe, with any accuracy, half-a-dozen of the men and women we had seen. Once the novelty of seeing people without clothes had worn off, the conditions in a Nudist community would be very much the same. True, the number met would be very much smaller and the newcomer would be much more observant under the unaccustomed circumstances, just as we notice the people more when we go abroad than we do at home; but in a very short time there would seem little difference between the clothed and the unclothed as far as personal reactions were concerned.

Let us try to see more clearly just how conceptions of physical beauty are likely to be affected by association with nudists. Men and women suffering from deformities sufficient to make their bodies repulsive would not wish to expose these deformities, and if they were so abnormal mentally or so unconscious of the repellent nature of their appearance as to try to join a reputable Nudist Society they would not be admitted. Such a society must, particularly at the present stage, exercise great discretion in the selection of members. It could hardly be expected, however, that they could carry discrimination so far as to exclude would-be members merely because they were short or tall, thin or fat. Since we are not shocked by seeing such people with their clothes on, the effect of seeing them without their clothes could not be very dreadful, and although we might not admire their physical appearance, we should probably soon become indifferent to it. The exposure to sun and air and the exercises which would be followed as a matter of course would inevitably cause a general improvement in physique. Muscles would be developed, poise would be acquired; and while those who were too

Right: *News Junkie.* Reading a copy of *The Naturist*, May 1945.

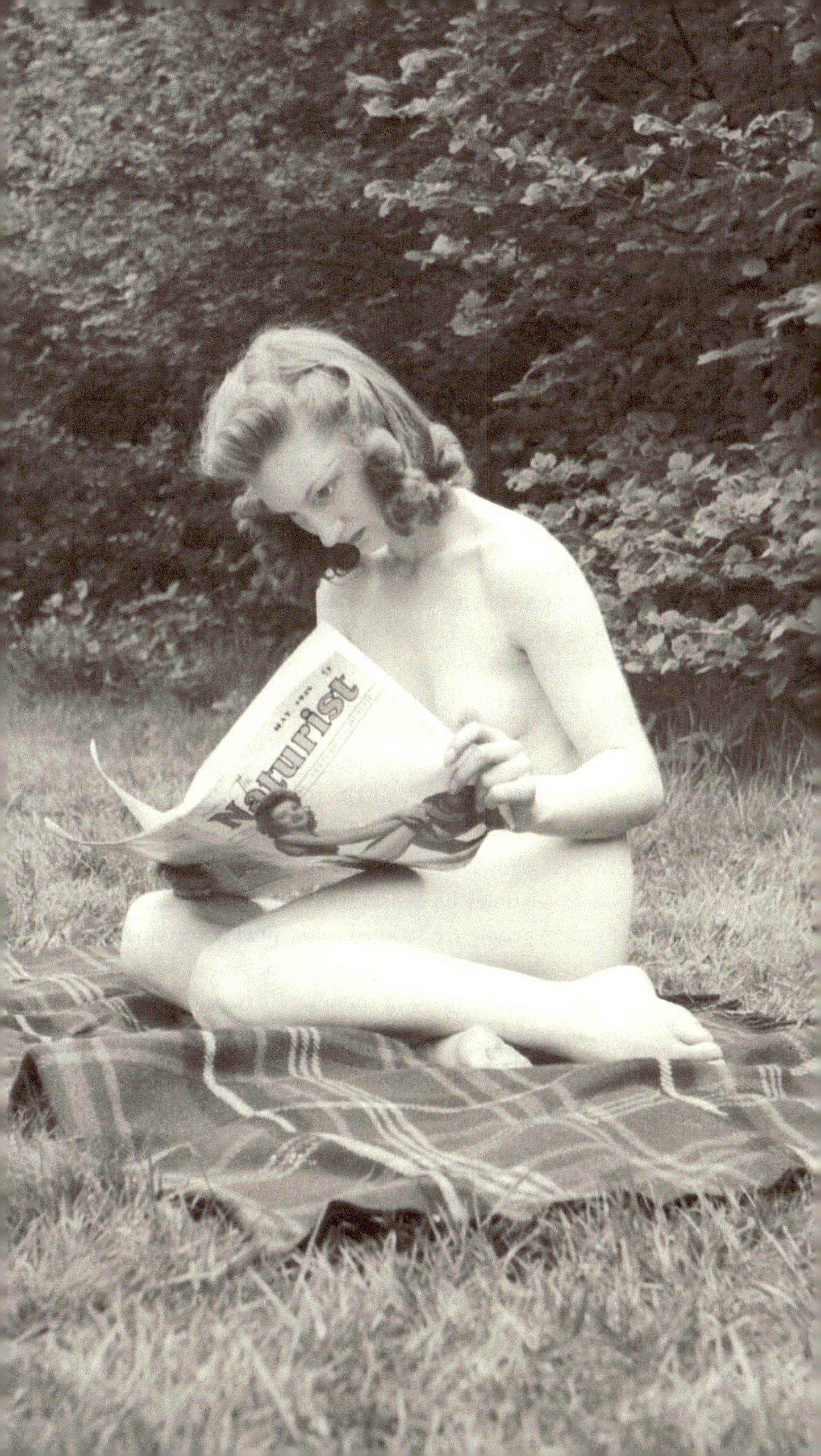

MAY 1950
Naturist

light would put on weight, those who had too much weight would reduce it. It is not fully realised by everyone that exercise actually does cause thin people to put on weight. This, no doubt, is partly because digestion and metabolism are improved, metabolism being the change from one substance into another which is performed in the body and by means of which all the cells of the body are built up. It is also partly because exercise develops muscle, which weighs considerably more than fat.

When discussing "The Psychological Point of View," we pointed out that vanity or self-respect would act as a stimulus towards improving the physique, and as a Nudist Association is sure to include a good many members of fine physique with a keenness for physical culture, there will be the greatest encouragement for the average member to acquire the shapeliness and grace which is possible to all individuals if they will only take the necessary steps. Here are example, opportunity and incentive to attain bodily beauties which otherwise might be, and generally are, ignored. The average standard of physique should, therefore, tend to rise constantly and should at all times be considerably higher than that with which most people are satisfied. Nor must we overlook the setting in which the nude bodies will be revealed. A naked man or woman in a drawing-room would be an incongruous sight, but transferred to a grassy dell with a background of trees or open sky they make quite a different picture. In such surroundings, a group composed of men, women and children engaged in a ball game, or rhythmical exercises under the direction of a skilled and experienced instructor, should satisfy the æsthetic requirements of any average onlooker.

Personal details of individuals become merged into the mass effect and none but a carping critic would pay much attention to them.

There is a big difference, too, between the dull whiteness of skin which has been deprived of its natural absorptions from sun and air, and the rich, golden brown of skin which has been moderately exposed. The white skin may be compared to a plant which has been artificially "blanched," like celery, or accidentally deprived of light like a patch of grass which has had a board or sack left lying upon it for a few days. The "tanned" skin is almost like a form of clothing itself. It is pleasing to the eye and carries with it a subconscious impression of glowing health. A well-tanned body does not look "naked" in the same way that a plain white body does. The facial expression of a healthy, happy group, too, must not be forgotten. In the ordinary way, we receive our impressions more from faces than from bodies, and bright eyes, smiling lips and an expression of alertness and intelligence must affect our sense of the beautiful in the human being. And all these may be gained by healthy exposure and exercise.

We cannot expect that the practice of Nudism will transform us all into Greek Gods and Goddesses, or that an ordinary nudist gathering will be as gratifying to our desires for beauty as a picture or piece of sculpture by one of the great masters. We must give the Nudists the credit for wishing to improve their own bodies and to encourage similar wishes in others; but they are just ordinary people, after all, even if their notions may seem somewhat eccentric to the uninitiated. One may visit a Nudist park with the hope of seeing beautiful human bodies in picturesque surroundings and enjoying the harmony of graceful gestures—and not be disappointed; but if we go to any exhibition of art, or attend a concert or variety show, we do not expect to find each item equal to the demands of our ideals, and we must be prepared to judge the Nudists from the "Æsthetic Point of View" with the same leniency that we are willing to extend to these.

CHAPTER VI

The Commonsense Point of View

NOW LET US REVIEW, from the "Commonsense Point of View," all that has been said in the preceding chapters. In the light of the facts stated and the deduction to be drawn from those facts, let us apply the practical logic which we should employ in solving one of the problems of everyday life, with which we are constantly confronted.

In Chapter I we have seen how the idea of wearing clothes originated and developed; how, starting from a practical basis, it subsequently became a convention—a convention that was, and still is, modified according to time and place. For practical purposes, protection of the body, it is undoubtedly more necessary now than it was in the beginning, because after so many generations of clothes-wearing our bodies are less capable of self-protection than they were in primitive times.

Our bodies now require protection not only from cold but also from excessive heat; and even if we hardened ourselves to such an extent that we could withstand the vagaries of the British climate, we still could not walk about the streets or frequent public places in a nude state. It would not only be unconventional, it would be illegal. The first policeman we met would "run us in." And this is quite right, too. If in addition to hardening our bodies we had broadened our minds to such an extent that we could face our fellow human beings without shame or self-consciousness, it would be wrong to forget that the less broad-minded people we met might find our conduct offensive. The law and social conventions both allow a certain amount of individual freedom, but they exist for the benefit of the community in general, "the greatest good of the greatest number," and if we break them in one way, other people may break them in other ways—ways very unpleasant for ourselves.

For this reason alone, it is not only wrong, it is stupid to expose the naked body in public or where other people with different ideas may see. In law, it is no excuse to say that you exposed yourself upon your own property. Unless that property is reasonably screened, so that no outside person can see you without trespassing or taking particular pains to do so, you are liable to be prosecuted for unlawful and indecent exposure. No reasonable person should take exception to this. Probably no reasonable person would want to do such a thing in the ordinary way, but there are cases where the offenders have no opportunities of exposing their naked bodies in the open air privately, or, perhaps, feel they are safe from observation in a secluded cove on the seashore. If this is done, strict precaution should be taken to receive due warning of the approach of strangers who might be offended or inimical. This, surely, is a matter of commonsense.

Partial exposure on the seashore, or in country places, is mainly a matter of local convention. In some places, shorts for a man and slip and brassiere for a woman are quite in order; in others, they are frowned upon by the authorities. In neither case, apparently, is public opinion consulted.

Linked up with this question of convention is the matter of morals, which we discussed in our second chapter. We hope we have made it quite clear that it is possible for the sexes to mix unclothed without an orgy of licentiousness taking place. There are, or were before Hitler extended the German cult of "Verboten" to almost Gilbertian lengths, about three million members of German Nudist Societies, all taking themselves and their nakedness very seriously. The movement has grown rapidly in America, where there 'are over a score of official leagues having many minor organisations affiliated to them. There are over seventy districts in our own country where "sun-bathing" groups are established, and the patroness of one of the largest is a British Countess. It would be distressing to think that all these people are immoral and that nothing is being attempted to check their immorality. A small proportion of them may be set down as "cranks." At some camps or parks the only food obtainable is strictly vegetarian; in some of the "Back to Nature" groups, it is regarded as heresy to eat any but uncooked foods, such as fruits and vegetables, and a ban on tobacco and alcohol is fairly general. All this may seem silly, but it is not immoral.

There is more reason in the nudist contention that free association without clothes is likely to lead to a better understanding of sex and to dispel the curiosity and furtiveness, which is so often the primary cause of immoral relations. This applies more particularly, of course, to children and young men and women. It has even been argued against nudism that it might destroy the glamour and excitement of sex and so lead either to complete indifference or at least to considerable decreased enjoyment of sexual relationship.

This argument must be founded on the mistaken idea that the nude body acts as an erotic stimulant. We have already explained that this is not so natural, and it can only be made to serve this purpose by the association of ideas and by partial draping or other artificial means.

With regard to health, the benefit to be obtained by "sun-bathing" in the conventional sense—that is, clothed in a bathing costume or such covering as may be called for in public—is so generally accepted, even though it is not generally understood that we hardly need consider this further; but, to avoid confusion, we may emphasise some of the points referred to in Chapter III.

It is not only "sun" which imparts this benefit. All light helps to stimulate the action of the skin and so is beneficial to the whole body. The rays most valuable in a general sense are the ultra-violet rays, and these are received in greater degree from the sun or from a lamp constructed to emit them. The ultra-violet rays will not penetrate clothing, so that any part of the body which is clothed is deprived of these rays. Modulated exposure over a large area is of more value than the concentrated exposure of a particular part—except in the case of medical treatment for the cure of some specific disease. Rays absorbed by the sexual organs benefit the whole of the body by stimulating "endocrine" secretions which are absorbed directly into the blood and so increase the vitality of all other organs. This is the strongest argument in favour of complete exposure, although such exposure may be made in strict privacy where such privacy is accompanied by the necessary facilities. Lamps and treatment by lamps are expensive and beyond the means of the majority; opportunities for complete exposure to natural sunlight are also restricted and beyond the reach of most people unless they combine with others in an organised group.

And it is not only light which the body requires, but air. Even exposure indoors with an ordinary coal fire is better than no exposure at all, and if carried out regularly will undoubtedly prove advantageous to health, although immediate and spectacular results must not be expected. Systematic exercise can be carried out in the same way, but cannot be quite so effective as when enjoyed in the open air with a perfectly free body in company with enthusiasts and under the supervision of a fully qualified director.

From the "Psychological Point of View" it is more difficult to generalise; in fact, one cannot generalise with any safety. The personal reactions of any given individual are liable to vary in so many respects from other individuals that effects from one cause may be totally opposite. A picture, a piece of music, even food, which delights some persons will be most distasteful to others, and where some may enjoy the freedom and friendliness of a Nudist group, others may feel ill at ease or definitely antagonistic. Before any benefit can be derived from such an association, it is necessary to free oneself entirely from all forms of prejudice. This is not easy for the average individual. Inherited tendencies, early training and regular environment are powerful influences which debar most of us from really "being ourselves."

Whatever it may be like in a few years' time, Nudism at present is so contrary to preconceived ideas that it is rather startling to contemplate with a view to personal participation. In the abstract and from a purely logical standpoint,

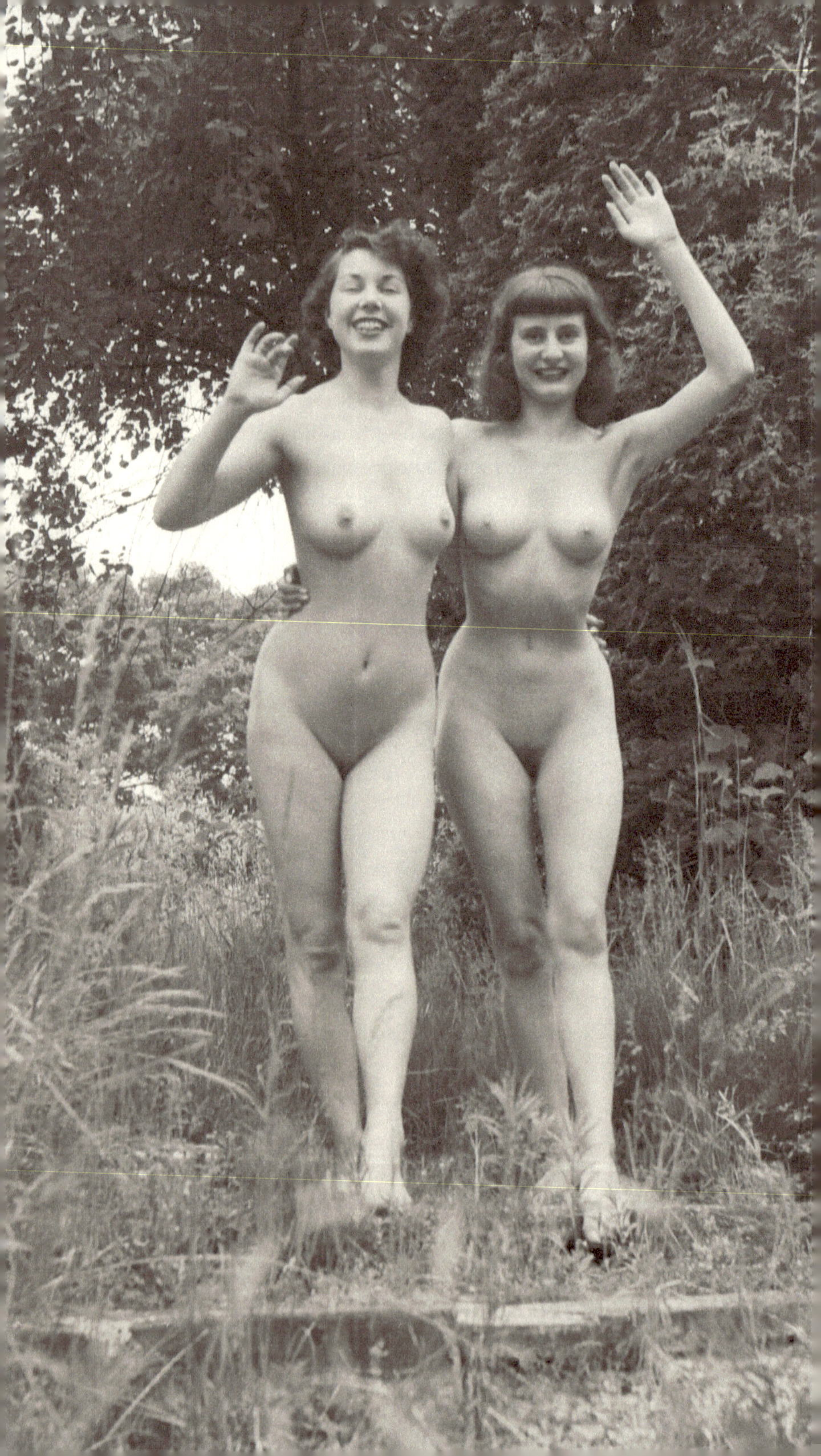

there is nothing objectionable about Nudism, providing that it is not obtruded upon non-nudists. Put colloquially, it is "all right for those who like it;" but its appeal, although growing, is never likely to be universal.

We hope the facts we have given will render the reader free from prejudices and misunderstandings and able to view the whole subject from a "Commonsense Point of View," but the final judgment must be a personal one dependent upon purely personal factors. This applies more forcibly, perhaps, to the last chapter, which, dealing with æsthetics, is also mainly psychological.

Whether one be exalted by the sight of a perfectly proportioned human being or revolted by the sight of physical imperfections is a personal matter. The very small proportion of people who visit our public art galleries would suggest that we are not, as a nation, obsessed by a love of the beautiful; on the other hand, ugly buildings and statues—and we have plenty of them in London alone seem to arouse very little protest. As a means of increasing the beauty of the human body, nudism deserves the encouragement of those who love beauty, but it would be foolish to become a nudist for that reason alone. And it would be undesirable, too, for Nudist groups to attract exhibitionists or Narcissists who are in love with their own beauty.

In conclusion, let us remind the reader that the wearing of clothes is a convention—a convention of very practical value up to a point, yet not unassailable any more than past conventions which have become obsolete. That Nudism does

---

Left: *Sunny Salutations.* Peggy Philips and Dana St. Clare.

offer a definite aid to health and happiness, and that there is
nothing immoral or decadent about the people who practise it. That the best way to consider Nudism, like any other
movement, is from the "Commonsense Point of View," and
if all that has been said in these pages is considered impar-
tially, it should be apparent that intelligent and respectable
people of both sexes can, under suitable conditions, benefit
by being "Naked and Unashamed."

The End

WOLFBAIT
UNDER THE COUNTER CULTURE

ALSO AVAILABLE

Cinema au Naturel
A history of nudist film.

Miniten: Rules of the Game
Invented in the 1930s, Miniten is
a tennis-like game played by naturists.

Naked as Nature Intended
The epic tale of a nudist picture by Pamela Green, with
photographs by Douglas "Dambuster" Webb, DFM.

The Naked Truth About Harrison Marks
The notorious biography by Franklyn Wood.

Past Masters of the Nude
An illustrated bibliography of nude photography books
published in England from 1896 to 1960.

Slide Show
A luscious look at the photographic
slides of Harrison Marks.

X-ray Specs and Other Vintage Ads
A unique treasure chest of vintage advertising,
full of tease and prurient silliness.

Doing Rude Things
The history of the British sex film.

THE STEPHEN GLASS COLLECTION

Amazons of Yesteryear
A rare, action-packed collection of images of wrestling
women of the 1940s and 1950s.

Beauty Off-Duty
Relaxed, everyday moments caught on camera.

Naked in the Menagerie
A playful look at Eve accompanied by her animal friends.

Nudist Camp Follies – volumes 1 and 2
An intimate look at the natural
and free atmosphere in Sun Clubs.

Nymphs and Naiads
Beauty unadorned and outdoors.

Poise and Pose
A magnificent series of photographs
of female beauty taken in the studio.

THE EVA GRANT COLLECTION

The Glamour Camera of Eva Grant
A short biography of Eva Grant, one of the world's foremost female figure photographers of the 1950s and 1960s, accompanied by a selection of some of her most enticing work.

Line and Form
A nostalgic review of Eva Grant's glamour magazine of the 1950s.

Glamour Model Revue
Featuring June Palmer, Paula Page and Tina Madison.

THE WILLIAM WELBY COLLECTION

Naked and Unashamed:
Nudism from Six Points of View
William Welby's initial impressions of nudism.

The Naked Truth about Nudism
William Welby gets to bare all in this firsthand exploration of British Naturism.

It's Only Natural: The Philosophy of Nudism
William Welby's musings on getting back to nature and the tyranny of fashion.

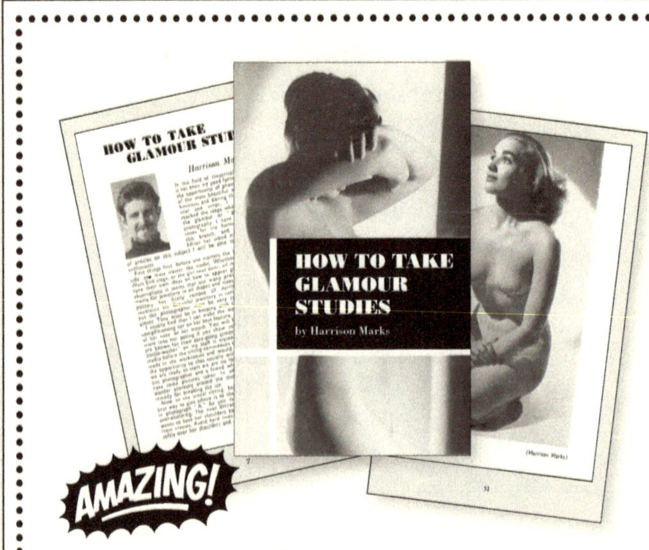

HOW TO TAKE GLAMOUR STUDIES
by Harrison Marks

www.ingramcontent.com/pod-product-compliance
Lightning Source LLC
Chambersburg PA
CBHW021826090726
47818CB00077BA/63